SMOOTHIE DIVERTICULITIS

The Essential Quick and Easy Fruit Blends Recipe Guide to Help Relieve Abdominal Pain and Support Digestive Health.

AVELINE WINTER

Copyright © 2024 Aveline Winter All rights reserved.

The information in this book is for general informational purposes only. The author and publisher are not liable for any damages or losses resulting from the use or misuse of the information provided.

TABLE OF CONTENT

INTRODUCTION 5

A Guide to Diverticulitis-Friendly Smoothies, Substitutes, and Pro Tips for Gentle Digestion. 6

Recipe 1: Banana Bliss Burst 9

Recipe 2: Peachy Keen Delight 12

Recipe 3: Mango Tango Elixir 14

Recipe 4: Berry Serenity Smoothie 16

Recipe 5: Vanilla Velvet Fusion 18

Recipe 6: Melon Marvel Mixer 21

Recipe 7: Apple Pie Pleasure 24

Recipe 8: Cucumber Mint Refresher 26

Recipe 9: Cherry Blossom Bliss 29

Recipe 10: Pineapple Mint Medley 31

Recipe 11: Pear Perfection Fusion 34

Recipe 12: Apricot Dream Delight 36

Recipe 13: Pineapple Passion Harmony 39

Recipe 14: Blue Sky Berry Blend 42

Recipe 15: Carrot Cake Concoction 45

Recipe 16: Gingered Pear Purity 48

Recipe 17: Cocoa Banana Bliss 51

Recipe 18: Plum Perfect Symphony 54

Recipe 19: Turmeric Ginger Tranquility 57
Recipe 20: Cinnamon Apple Delight 60
CONCLUSION 63

INTRODUCTION

Welcome to *"Smoothies for Diverticulitis"* – a thoughtful guide born out of empathy for those navigating the challenges of digestive health. Understanding the meticulous choices required in meal planning for individuals with diverticulitis, I've witnessed the struggles many face. This book is a testament to my commitment to make this journey more manageable.

Inside, you'll discover a collection of carefully crafted smoothie recipes tailored to ease the digestive burden associated with diverticulitis. Packed with essential nutrients, these smoothies aim to provide not just sustenance but a delightful experience for your taste buds.

By delving into this book, you're embracing a resource designed to alleviate your dietary concerns. Uncover a plethora of benefits, from promoting gut health to enhancing nutrient absorption. Each page is a step toward embracing a tasteful and nourishing solution to your dietary challenges.

Don't miss out on the opportunity to transform your relationship with food and take charge of your well-being. The journey to digestive wellness begins here, within the pages of "Smoothies for Diverticulitis."

A Guide to Diverticulitis-Friendly Smoothies, Substitutes, and Pro Tips for Gentle Digestion.

Below is a comprehensive guide of ingredients, substitutes, and pro tips for smoothies that nourish and soothe.

What To Avoid:
1. Seeds and Nuts: Those little crunchy bits might seem harmless, but for diverticulitis warriors, they can be trouble. Skip the chia seeds, flaxseeds, and nuts to keep things smooth.

2. Raw Greens with Fibrous Stalks: Tough fiber from kale or celery can be hard to digest. Opt for softer greens like spinach and remove those celery strings before blending.

3. Citrus with Pulp: Citrus fruits can be acidic and the pulp might irritate. Go for peeled and deseeded citrus like oranges or opt for less acidic fruits.

4. High-Fiber Fruits with Skin: The skin of fruits like apples or pears can be a bit too much. Peel them before tossing into the blender.

Ingredient Substitutes:
1. Flaxseed Meal or Nut Butters: Instead of whole seeds or nuts, go for flaxseed meal or nut butters. They give you the flavor without the crunch.

2. Cooked Greens: Lightly steam or cook tougher greens like kale or collard greens to make them gentler on the stomach.

3. Citrus Juice without Pulp: Freshly squeezed citrus juice without the pulp is a tasty alternative. You get the zing without the potential irritation.

4. Fruit Purees: Opt for peeled and deseeded fruits or use fruit purees. They're gentler on digestion while keeping the fruity goodness.

Pro Tips:

- **Protein Boost:** Add protein sources like Greek yogurt or protein powder to your smoothies. It helps maintain energy levels and aids in recovery.

- **Hydration is Key:** Include hydrating elements like coconut water or aloe vera juice to keep things refreshing and easy on the stomach.

- **Mind the Temperature:** Cold or icy drinks might not sit well, so consider room temperature or slightly chilled smoothies.

Remember, everyone's stomach is a bit different, so it's always a good idea to test and adjust based on individual reactions. Cheers to blending up some gut-friendly goodness!

GUT-FRIENDLY SMOOTHIE GOODNESS JUST FOR YOU!

Recipe 1: Banana Bliss Burst

Introduction:

Indulge in the Banana Bliss Burst – a smoothie designed with care for those navigating diverticulitis. This velvety blend of banana, low-fat yogurt, and skim milk not only tantalizes your taste buds but also serves as a soothing elixir for your digestive wellness.

Ingredients:
1. 1 ripe Banana
2. 1/2 cup Low-fat Yogurt
3. 1 cup Skim Milk

Instructions:

1. Peel and Slice the Banana:
  - Peel a ripe banana and slice it into smaller pieces for easier blending.

2. Combine Ingredients in Blender:
  - In a blender, add the banana slices, low-fat yogurt, and skim milk.

3. Blend to Creaminess:
- Blend the ingredients on high until you achieve a smooth and creamy consistency. This usually takes about 1-2 minutes.

4. Texture Adjustment:
- Check the smoothie's texture and adjust by adding more skim milk if you desire a thinner consistency.

5. Serve Fresh:
- Pour the Banana Bliss Burst into a glass, and relish its creamy goodness immediately.

Health Benefits for Diverticulitis:

- **Bananas Soluble Fiber:** Bananas are rich in soluble fiber, aiding in softening stools and promoting regular bowel movements, which can be beneficial for diverticulitis management.

- **Gut-Friendly Yogurt:** Low-fat yogurt contributes probiotics, supporting a healthy gut environment and potentially easing digestive discomfort.

- **Low-Fat Skim Milk:** Skim milk adds a creamy texture without the excess fat, providing a source of calcium and protein that's gentle on the digestive system.

The Banana Bliss Burst is not just a treat for your palate but a thoughtful combination curated to provide comfort and nourishment for those with diverticulitis. Enjoy this smoothie as a delightful addition to your wellness routine.

Recipe 2: Peachy Keen Delight

Introduction:
The Peachy Keen Delight – a luscious smoothie tailored for individuals managing diverticulitis. Immerse yourself in the goodness of peach slices, low-fat Greek yogurt, and almond milk, creating a delightful blend that not only satisfies your taste buds but also nurtures your digestive health.

Ingredients:
1. 1 cup Peach Slices (fresh or frozen)
2. 1/2 cup Low-fat Greek Yogurt
3. 1 cup Almond Milk

Instructions:
1. Prepare the Peaches:
   - If using fresh peaches, peel and slice them. For frozen peaches, allow them to thaw slightly.
2. Combine Ingredients in Blender:
   - In a blender, add the peach slices, low-fat Greek yogurt, and almond milk.
3. Blend to Silky Smoothness:
   - Blend the ingredients on high speed until the mixture turns into a silky and smooth texture, typically taking about 1-2 minutes.

4. Check Consistency:
   - Assess the consistency of the smoothie and adjust by adding more almond milk if a thinner texture is preferred.

5. Serve with Elegance:
   - Pour the Peachy Keen Delight into a glass, and savor its elegant flavors. Consider garnishing with a peach slice for a touch of sophistication.

Health Benefits for Diverticulitis:

- **Peach's Dietary Fiber:** Peaches contribute dietary fiber, aiding in digestion and promoting regular bowel movements, which is beneficial for diverticulitis patients.
- **Probiotic-Rich Greek Yogurt:** Low-fat Greek yogurt introduces probiotics to the mix, supporting gut health and potentially alleviating digestive discomfort.
- **Nutrient-Rich Almond Milk:** Almond milk provides a nutrient boost without the lactose, offering vitamins and minerals while being gentle on the digestive system.

The Peachy Keen Delight is not just a treat for your senses but a crafted blend designed to enhance your well-being while managing diverticulitis. Enjoy the delightful fusion of flavors and health benefits in every sip.

Recipe 3: Mango Tango Elixir

Introduction:
Welcome to the Mango Tango Elixir – a delightful smoothie specially crafted for individuals managing diverticulitis. This vibrant concoction not only satisfies your taste buds but also supports your digestive health. Packed with the goodness of mango chunks, low-fat cottage cheese, and hydrating coconut water, this smoothie is a refreshing way to nurture your body.

Ingredients:
1. 1 cup Mango chunks (fresh or frozen)
2. 1/2 cup Low-fat Cottage Cheese
3. 1 cup Coconut Water

Instructions:

1. Prepare the Mango:
   - If using fresh mango, peel and dice it into chunks. If using frozen mango, allow it to thaw slightly for easier blending.

2. Combine Ingredients in Blender:
   - In a blender, add the mango chunks, low-fat cottage cheese, and coconut water.

3. Blend to Perfection:
   - Blend all ingredients on high speed until you achieve a smooth and creamy consistency. This might take about 1-2 minutes.

4. Check and Adjust:
 - Taste the smoothie and adjust the texture or sweetness by adding more coconut water or mango if necessary.

5. Serve Chilled:
 - Pour the Mango Tango Elixir into a glass and refrigerate or add ice cubes for a refreshing chill.

Health Benefits for Diverticulitis:
- **Fiber-Rich Mango:** Mango is a great source of dietary fiber, which helps in promoting regular bowel movements and preventing constipation, a common concern for diverticulitis patients.

- **Protein-Packed Cottage Cheese:** Low-fat cottage cheese adds a protein boost, supporting muscle health and providing a nutrient-dense element to the smoothie.

- **Hydrating Coconut Water:** Coconut water not only enhances the drink's taste but also provides hydration, vital for maintaining a healthy digestive system.

This Mango Tango Elixir is not only a treat for your taste buds but a thoughtful blend tailored to nourish and support individuals managing diverticulitis, making it a delightful addition to your daily routine.

Recipe 4: Berry Serenity Smoothie

Introduction:

Embark on a serene journey with the Berry Serenity Smoothie – a refreshing blend thoughtfully crafted for those navigating diverticulitis. Immerse yourself in the antioxidant-rich allure of blueberries, the probiotic goodness of low-fat kefir, and the plant-based harmony of soy milk. This smoothie not only tantalizes your taste buds but also nurtures your digestive well-being.

Ingredients:
1. 1 cup Blueberries (fresh or frozen)
2. 1/2 cup Low-fat Kefir
3. 1 cup Soy Milk

Instructions:

1. Prepare the Blueberries:
   - If using fresh blueberries, rinse them. For frozen blueberries, allow them to thaw slightly.

2. Combine Ingredients in Blender:
   - In a blender, add the blueberries, low-fat kefir, and soy milk.

3. Blend to Serenity:
   - Blend the ingredients on high until the mixture achieves a serene and smooth consistency, typically taking about 1-2 minutes.

4. Check and Adjust Texture:
   - Assess the texture of the smoothie and adjust by adding more soy milk if a thinner consistency is desired.

5. Serve Tranquility:
   - Pour the Berry Serenity Smoothie into a glass and savor its tranquil flavors. Consider garnishing with a few fresh blueberries for an extra burst of freshness.

Health Benefits for Diverticulitis:
- **Blueberries' Antioxidant Power:** Blueberries are rich in antioxidants, offering anti-inflammatory benefits that can be supportive for diverticulitis patients.

- **Probiotic-Rich Kefir:** Low-fat kefir introduces probiotics, aiding in maintaining a healthy balance of gut flora and potentially easing digestive discomfort.

- **Plant-Based Soy Milk:** Soy milk provides a plant-based alternative, offering a source of protein and essential nutrients without the potential irritants found in dairy.

The Berry Serenity Smoothie is more than a beverage; it's a blend designed to bring peace to your palate and support to your digestive wellness. Revel in the tranquility of this exquisite fusion of berries, kefir, and soy milk with each sip.

Recipe 5: Vanilla Velvet Fusion

Introduction:

Step into the world of soothing indulgence with the Vanilla Velvet Fusion – a velvety smoothie meticulously crafted for individuals managing diverticulitis. Enrich your senses with the gentle notes of vanilla yogurt, the tropical sweetness of pineapple chunks, and the creamy embrace of cashew milk. Beyond its delightful taste, this smoothie is tailored to support your digestive health.

Ingredients:

1. 1/2 cup Vanilla Yogurt (low-fat)
2. 1 cup Pineapple Chunks (fresh or frozen)
3. 1 cup Cashew Milk

Instructions:

1. Prepare the Pineapple:
   - If using fresh pineapple, peel and cut the pineapple into chunks. For frozen pineapple, allow it to thaw slightly.

2. Combine Ingredients in Blender:
   - In a blender, add the vanilla yogurt, pineapple chunks, and cashew milk.

3. Blend to Velvety Perfection:
- Blend the ingredients on high until the mixture reaches a velvety and smooth consistency, typically taking about 1-2 minutes.

4. Check and Adjust Creaminess:
   - Assess the creaminess of the smoothie and adjust by adding more cashew milk if desired.

5. Serve Luxuriously:
   - Pour the Vanilla Velvet Fusion into a glass and relish its luxurious flavors. Consider adding a pineapple chunk as a garnish for a touch of elegance.

Health Benefits for Diverticulitis:

- **Vanilla Yogurt's Digestive Comfort:** Vanilla yogurt offers a soothing quality, potentially easing digestive discomfort associated with diverticulitis.

- **Pineapple's Enzymes:** Pineapple contains enzymes like bromelain, which may assist in digestion and help reduce inflammation in the digestive tract.

- **Creamy Cashew Milk:** Cashew milk provides a creamy texture without the lactose, offering a source of healthy fats and nutrients that are gentle on the digestive system.

The Vanilla Velvet Fusion is not just a treat for your taste buds; it's a velvety embrace designed to bring comfort and support to individuals managing diverticulitis. Immerse yourself in the richness of this smoothie, celebrating the fusion of vanilla, pineapple, and cashew milk with each sip.

Recipe 6: Melon Marvel Mixer

Introduction:

Dive into a refreshing experience with the Melon Marvel Mixer – a splendid smoothie tailored for those navigating the nuances of diverticulitis. This blend combines the succulent sweetness of cantaloupe cubes, the probiotic richness of low-fat buttermilk, and the antioxidant power of unsweetened green tea. Beyond its delicious profile, this smoothie is a thoughtful addition to support digestive health.

Ingredients:
1. 1 cup Cantaloupe Cubes
2. 1/2 cup Low-fat Buttermilk
3. 1 cup Unsweetened Green Tea

Instructions:

1. Prepare the Cantaloupe:
   - Peel and cube the cantaloupe, ensuring to remove seeds for a smoother blend.

2. Brew Unsweetened Green Tea:
   - Prepare unsweetened green tea and allow it to cool to room temperature or chill in the refrigerator.

3. Combine Ingredients in Blender:
   - In a blender, add the cantaloupe cubes, low-fat buttermilk, and cooled unsweetened green tea.

4. Blend to Melon Marvel:
 - Blend the ingredients on high until the mixture achieves a marvelously smooth consistency, typically taking about 1-2 minutes.

5. Check and Adjust Temperature:
 - Assess the temperature of the smoothie and adjust by adding ice cubes or chilling in the refrigerator if a colder beverage is desired.

6. Serve with Delight:
 - Pour the Melon Marvel Mixer into a glass and revel in its delightful flavors. Consider garnishing with a cantaloupe wedge for an extra touch of elegance.

Health Benefits for Diverticulitis:

- Cantaloupe's Dietary Fiber: Cantaloupe contributes dietary fiber, aiding in digestion and promoting regular bowel movements, which is advantageous for diverticulitis patients.

- Probiotic-Rich Buttermilk: Low-fat buttermilk introduces probiotics, supporting a healthy balance of gut flora and potentially easing digestive discomfort.

- Antioxidant-Packed Green Tea: Unsweetened green tea provides antioxidants that may help reduce inflammation and contribute to overall digestive wellness.

The Melon Marvel Mixer isn't just a delicious blend; it's a tailored fusion crafted to bring joy and support to individuals managing diverticulitis. Savor the goodness of cantaloupe, buttermilk, and green tea with each sip, knowing you're nurturing your digestive health in a delightful way.

Recipe 7: Apple Pie Pleasure

Introduction:
Indulge in the comforting embrace of the Apple Pie Pleasure – a delightful smoothie designed with care for those journeying through diverticulitis. Immerse yourself in the wholesome goodness of peeled apple slices, the creamy richness of low-fat ricotta cheese, and the nutty essence of oat milk. Beyond its sweet charm, this smoothie is a heartwarming addition to support digestive wellness.

Ingredients:
1. 1 cup Apple Slices (peeled)
2. 1/2 cup Low-fat Ricotta Cheese
3. 1 cup Oat Milk

Instructions:

1. Prepare the Apples:
   - Peel and slice the apples, ensuring to remove seeds and cores for a smoother blend.

2. Combine Ingredients in Blender:
   - In a blender, add the peeled apple slices, low-fat ricotta cheese, and oat milk.

3. Blend to Apple Pie Bliss:
   - Blend the ingredients on high until the mixture attains a blissfully smooth consistency, usually taking about 1-2 minutes.

4. Check and Adjust Creaminess:
   - Assess the creaminess of the smoothie and adjust by adding more oat milk if a silkier texture is desired.

5. Serve with Warmth:
   - Pour the Apple Pie Pleasure into a glass and relish its warm, comforting flavors. Consider a sprinkle of cinnamon as a garnish for an extra touch of indulgence.

Health Benefits for Diverticulitis:
- **Apple's Soluble Fiber:** Apples are rich in soluble fiber, aiding in softening stools and promoting regular bowel movements, which can be beneficial for diverticulitis management.
- **Protein-Packed Ricotta Cheese:** Low-fat ricotta cheese adds a protein boost, supporting muscle health and providing a nutrient-dense element to the smoothie.
- **Nutrient-Rich Oat Milk:** Oat milk brings a nutty essence to the mix, offering essential nutrients and dietary fiber that are gentle on the digestive system.

The Apple Pie Pleasure isn't just a taste of sweetness; it's a crafted blend designed to bring comfort and nourishment to individuals managing diverticulitis. Enjoy the delightful fusion of apple slices, ricotta cheese, and oat milk with each sip, knowing you're nurturing your digestive health in the most pleasurable way.

Recipe 8: Cucumber Mint Refresher

Introduction:

Quench your thirst and invigorate your senses with the Cucumber Mint Refresher – a revitalizing smoothie thoughtfully crafted for those embracing the challenges of diverticulitis. Immerse yourself in the crispness of peeled cucumber slices, the invigorating essence of mint leaves, and the probiotic goodness of low-fat plain yogurt. Beyond its refreshing taste, this smoothie is a cool sip of support for your digestive well-being.

Ingredients:

1. 1 cup Cucumber Slices (peeled)
2. 1/4 cup Mint Leaves
3. 1/2 cup Low-fat Plain Yogurt

Instructions:

1. Prepare the Cucumbers:
  - Peel and slice the cucumbers, ensuring to remove seeds for a smoother blend.

2. Combine Ingredients in Blender:
  - In a blender, add the peeled cucumber slices, mint leaves, and low-fat plain yogurt.

3. Blend to Cool Perfection:
  - Blend the ingredients on high until the mixture achieves a refreshingly cool and smooth consistency, typically taking about 1-2 minutes.

4. Check and Adjust Minty Freshness:
  - Assess the minty freshness of the smoothie and adjust by adding more mint leaves if desired.

5. Serve Chilled Elegance:
  - Pour the Cucumber Mint Refresher into a glass and enjoy its chilled elegance. Consider garnishing with a mint sprig for a touch of sophistication.

Health Benefits for Diverticulitis:

- **Cucumber's Hydration and Fiber:** Cucumbers are hydrating and contain dietary fiber, contributing to improved digestion and hydration, which is beneficial for diverticulitis patients.

- **Mint's Digestive Comfort:** Mint leaves offer a soothing quality, potentially easing digestive discomfort associated with diverticulitis.

- **Probiotic-Rich Plain Yogurt:** Low-fat plain yogurt introduces probiotics, supporting a healthy gut environment and potentially alleviating digestive discomfort.

The Cucumber Mint Refresher is not just a drink; it's a revitalizing blend designed to bring a burst of freshness and support to individuals managing diverticulitis. Relish the cool fusion of cucumber, mint, and plain yogurt with each sip, knowing you're nurturing your digestive health in a refreshing way.

Recipe 9: Cherry Blossom Bliss

Introduction:
Embark on a journey of blissful flavors with the Cherry Blossom Bliss – a delectable smoothie created with care for those navigating diverticulitis. Immerse yourself in the sweetness of pitted cherries, the protein-rich embrace of low-fat cottage cheese, and the nutty essence of almond milk. Beyond its delightful taste, this smoothie is a thoughtfully crafted blend to support your digestive well-being.

Ingredients:
1. 1 cup Cherries (pitted)
2. 1/2 cup Low-fat Cottage Cheese
3. 1 cup Almond Milk

Instructions:
1. **Pit the Cherries:**
   - Remove pits from the cherries for a smoother blend.
2. **Combine Ingredients in Blender:**
   - In a blender, add the pitted cherries, low-fat cottage cheese, and almond milk.
3. **Blend to Blossom Perfection:**
   - Blend the ingredients on high until the mixture achieves a perfectly smooth and blissful consistency, typically taking about 1-2 minutes.

4. Check and Adjust Creaminess:
   - Assess the creaminess of the smoothie and adjust by adding more almond milk if a silkier texture is desired.

5. Serve with Cherry Elegance:
   - Pour the Cherry Blossom Bliss into a glass and savor its elegant flavors. Consider garnishing with a cherry on top for an extra touch of delight.

Health Benefits for Diverticulitis:
- **Cherry's Antioxidant Power:** Cherries are rich in antioxidants, offering anti-inflammatory benefits that can be supportive for diverticulitis patients.

- **Protein-Packed Cottage Cheese:** Low-fat cottage cheese adds a protein boost, supporting muscle health and providing a nutrient-dense element to the smoothie.

- **Nutty Almond Milk:** Almond milk provides a nutty essence to the mix, offering essential nutrients and dietary fiber that are gentle on the digestive system.

The Cherry Blossom Bliss is more than a treat for your taste buds; it's a curated blend designed to bring joy and support to individuals managing diverticulitis. Enjoy the delightful fusion of cherries, cottage cheese, and almond milk with each sip, knowing you're nurturing your digestive health in a blissful way.

Recipe 10: Pineapple Mint Medley

Introduction:
The Pineapple Mint Medley – a refreshing smoothie crafted for those seeking digestive support. Revel in the tropical sweetness of pineapple chunks, the invigorating touch of fresh mint leaves, the creaminess of low-fat yogurt, and the nutty essence of almond milk. This medley not only tantalizes your taste buds but also brings a burst of nourishment to those managing diverticulitis.

Ingredients:
1. 1 cup Pineapple Chunks
2. 1/4 cup Fresh Mint Leaves
3. 1/2 cup Low-fat Yogurt
4. 1 cup Almond Milk

Instructions:
1. Prepare the Pineapple:
   - Cut fresh pineapple into chunks, ensuring to remove the core for smoother blending.

2. Add Fresh Mint:
   - In a blender, combine the pineapple chunks and fresh mint leaves.

3. Include Low-Fat Yogurt:
   - Add the low-fat yogurt to the blender for a creamy and rich texture.

4. Pour in Almond Milk:
 - Pour the almond milk into the blender to infuse a nutty essence into the smoothie.

5. Blend to Medley Harmony:
 - Blend the ingredients on high speed until the mixture achieves a harmonious and smooth consistency. This typically takes about 1-2 minutes.

6. Check and Adjust Freshness:
 - Assess the freshness of the smoothie and adjust by adding more mint leaves if desired.

7. Serve with Tropical Bliss:
 - Pour the Pineapple Mint Medley into a glass and relish its tropical bliss. Consider garnishing with a mint sprig for a touch of visual appeal.

Health Benefits for Diverticulitis:

- Pineapple's Enzymes: Pineapple contains enzymes like bromelain, aiding digestion and potentially reducing inflammation in the digestive tract.

- Mint's Digestive Comfort: Mint leaves offer a soothing quality, potentially easing digestive discomfort associated with diverticulitis.

- Probiotic-Rich Yogurt: Low-fat yogurt introduces probiotics, supporting a healthy balance of gut flora and potentially alleviating digestive discomfort.

- **Nutty Almond Milk:** Almond milk provides a nutty essence to the mix, offering essential nutrients and dietary fiber that are gentle on the digestive system.

The Pineapple Mint Medley is more than a refreshing beverage; it's a carefully blended symphony of flavors designed to bring joy and nourishment to individuals managing diverticulitis. Enjoy the delightful fusion of pineapple, mint, yogurt, and almond milk with each sip, knowing you're embracing a medley of goodness for your digestive health.

Recipe 11: Pear Perfection Fusion

Introduction:

The Pear Perfection Fusion – a velvety smoothie crafted for those navigating the nuances of diverticulitis. Immerse yourself in the natural sweetness of a ripe, peeled pear, the protein-rich embrace of low-fat Greek yogurt, and the creamy allure of cashew milk. Beyond its delectable taste, this smoothie is a thoughtful blend to support digestive wellness.

Ingredients:
1. 1 Ripe Pear (peeled)
2. 1/2 cup Low-fat Greek Yogurt
3. 1 cup Cashew Milk

Instructions:

1. Prepare the Pear:
   - Peel and dice a ripe pear, removing the core for a smoother blend.

2. Combine Ingredients in Blender:
   - In a blender, add the peeled pear chunks, low-fat Greek yogurt, and cashew milk.

3. Blend to Perfection:
   - Blend the ingredients on high until the mixture achieves a velvety and smooth consistency, typically taking about 1-2 minutes.

4. Check and Adjust Creaminess:
   - Assess the creaminess of the smoothie and adjust by adding more cashew milk if a silkier texture is desired.

5. Serve with Elegance:
   - Pour the Pear Perfection Fusion into a glass and relish its elegant flavors. Consider garnishing with a pear slice for an extra touch of sophistication.

Health Benefits for Diverticulitis:
- **Pear's Soluble Fiber:** Pears are rich in soluble fiber, aiding in softening stools and promoting regular bowel movements, which is beneficial for diverticulitis management.
- **Probiotic-Rich Greek Yogurt:** Low-fat Greek yogurt introduces probiotics, supporting gut health and potentially easing digestive discomfort.
- **Creamy Cashew Milk:** Cashew milk provides a creamy texture without the lactose, offering a source of healthy fats and nutrients that are gentle on the digestive system.

The Pear Perfection Fusion is more than a delightful sip; it's a carefully curated blend designed to bring joy and support to individuals managing diverticulitis. Enjoy the harmonious fusion of ripe pear, Greek yogurt, and cashew milk with each sip, knowing you're nurturing your digestive health in a perfect way.

Recipe 12: Apricot Dream Delight

Introduction:

Savor a dreamy escape with the Apricot Dream Delight – a velvety smoothie meticulously crafted for those embracing the journey of diverticulitis. Immerse yourself in the natural sweetness of pitted apricot halves, the comforting allure of low-fat vanilla yogurt, and the nutty richness of soy milk. Beyond its delightful taste, this smoothie is a thoughtful blend designed to bring a touch of bliss to your digestive well-being.

Ingredients:

1. 1 cup Apricot Halves (pitted)
2. 1/2 cup Low-fat Vanilla Yogurt
3. 1 cup Soy Milk

Instructions:

1. Prepare the Apricots:
   - Ensure apricots are pitted, and if desired, slice them for easier blending.

2. Combine Ingredients in Blender:
   - In a blender, add the pitted apricot halves, a generous scoop of low-fat vanilla yogurt, and soy milk.

3. Blend to Dreamy Consistency:
   - Blend the ingredients on high until the mixture achieves a dreamy and smooth consistency, typically taking about 1-2 minutes.

4. Check and Adjust Creaminess:
   - Assess the creaminess of the smoothie and adjust by adding more soy milk if a silkier texture is desired.

5. Serve with Delight:
   - Pour the Apricot Dream Delight into a glass and savor its delightful flavors. Consider a sprinkle of cinnamon or an apricot slice as a garnish for an extra touch of elegance.

Health Benefits for Diverticulitis:
- **Apricot's Dietary Fiber:** Apricots are a good source of dietary fiber, aiding in digestion and promoting regular bowel movements, which is beneficial for diverticulitis management.

- **Vanilla Yogurt's Digestive Comfort:** Low-fat vanilla yogurt offers a soothing quality, potentially easing digestive discomfort associated with diverticulitis.

- **Nutty Soy Milk:** Soy milk provides a nutty richness to the mix, offering essential nutrients and dietary fiber that are gentle on the digestive system.

The Apricot Dream Delight is not just a taste of sweetness; it's a curated blend designed to bring joy and support to individuals managing diverticulitis. Enjoy the delightful fusion of apricot, vanilla yogurt, and soy milk with each sip, knowing you're nurturing your digestive health in a dreamy way.

Recipe 13: Pineapple Passion Harmony

Introduction:
Embark on a harmonious journey with the Pineapple Passion Harmony – a velvety smoothie tailored for those navigating diverticulitis. Immerse yourself in the tropical sweetness of pineapple chunks, the protein-rich embrace of low-fat ricotta cheese, and the nutty essence of almond milk. Beyond its delightful taste, this smoothie is a thoughtfully crafted blend designed to bring a touch of passion to your digestive well-being.

Ingredients:
1. 1 cup Pineapple Chunks
2. 1/2 cup Low-fat Ricotta Cheese
3. 1 cup Almond Milk

Instructions:
1. Prepare the Pineapple:
   - Cut fresh pineapple into chunks, ensuring to remove the core for smoother blending.
2. Combine Ingredients in Blender:
   - In a blender, add the pineapple chunks, a generous dollop of low-fat ricotta cheese, and almond milk.

3. Blend to Harmonious Consistency
- Blend the ingredients on high until the mixture achieves a harmonious and smooth consistency, typically taking about 1-2 minutes.

4. Check and Adjust Creaminess:
- Assess the creaminess of the smoothie and adjust by adding more almond milk if a silkier texture is desired.

5. Serve with Passionate Joy:
- Pour the Pineapple Passion Harmony into a glass and savor its passionate flavors. Consider garnishing with a pineapple wedge for an extra touch of elegance.

Health Benefits for Diverticulitis:
- **Pineapple's Enzymes:** Pineapple contains enzymes like bromelain, aiding digestion and potentially reducing inflammation in the digestive tract.

- **Protein-Packed Ricotta Cheese:** Low-fat ricotta cheese adds a protein boost, supporting muscle health and providing a nutrient-dense element to the smoothie.

- **Nutty Almond Milk:** Almond milk provides a nutty essence to the mix, offering essential nutrients and dietary fiber that are gentle on the digestive system.

The Pineapple Passion Harmony is more than a tropical escape; it's a carefully curated blend designed to bring joy and support to individuals managing diverticulitis. Enjoy the delightful fusion of pineapple, ricotta cheese, and almond milk with each sip, knowing you're nurturing your digestive health in a harmonious way.

Recipe 14: Blue Sky Berry Blend

Introduction:

The Blue Sky Berry Blend – a meticulously crafted smoothie tailored for those tending to the nuances of diverticulitis. This delightful blend combines the antioxidant-rich allure of blueberries, the probiotic goodness of low-fat kefir, and the creamy embrace of cashew milk. More than just a flavorful treat, this smoothie is thoughtfully designed to bring both joy and nourishment to individuals seeking digestive well-being.

Ingredients:
- 1 cup Blueberries (fresh or frozen)
- 1/2 cup Low-fat Kefir
- 1 cup Cashew Milk

Instructions:

1. Prepare the Blueberries:
   - Rinse 1 cup of fresh blueberries under cold water or thaw frozen blueberries, ensuring they are ready for blending.

2. Combine Ingredients in Blender:
   - In a blender, add the prepared blueberries, 1/2 cup of low-fat kefir, and 1 cup of cashew milk.

3. Blend to Sky-High Consistency:
- Secure the blender lid and blend the ingredients on high speed until the mixture achieves a smooth and sky-high consistency. This usually takes about 1-2 minutes.

4. Check and Adjust Creaminess:
 - Pause and check the creaminess of the smoothie. If a silkier texture is desired, add more cashew milk gradually and blend again.

5. Serve with Berry Bliss:
 - Pour the Blue Sky Berry Blend into a glass, embracing the vibrant hues. Consider garnishing with a sprinkle of chia seeds or a few whole blueberries for an extra burst of goodness.

Health Benefits for Diverticulitis:
- **Blueberries' Antioxidant Power:** Rich in antioxidants, blueberries may provide anti-inflammatory benefits that can support diverticulitis patients by easing inflammation in the digestive tract.

- **Probiotic-Rich Kefir:** Low-fat kefir introduces probiotics, fostering a healthy balance of gut flora. This can be particularly beneficial for diverticulitis patients, potentially alleviating digestive discomfort.

- **Creamy Cashew Milk:** Cashew milk, with its creamy texture and nutrient content, serves as a gentle source of healthy fats and essential nutrients that can be soothing to the digestive system.

The Blue Sky Berry Blend isn't just a delightful mix of flavors; it's a healthful choice crafted to bring vitality and support to individuals managing diverticulitis. Enjoy the refreshing fusion of blueberries, kefir, and cashew milk with each sip, knowing you're nurturing your digestive health beneath the serene blue sky.

Recipe 15: Carrot Cake Concoction

Introduction:
The Carrot Cake Concoction – a velvety smoothie designed to bring joy and digestive support to those managing diverticulitis. This delightful blend features the sweetness of cooked and cooled carrots, the probiotic richness of low-fat plain yogurt, and the nutty essence of almond milk. Beyond its indulgent taste, this smoothie is a thoughtful creation aimed at nurturing your digestive well-being.

Ingredients:
1. 1 cup Cooked and Cooled Carrots
2. 1/2 cup Low-fat Plain Yogurt
3. 1 cup Almond Milk

Instructions:
1. Prepare the Carrots:
   - Cook fresh carrots until tender, then allow them to cool. Measure 1 cup of these cooked and cooled carrots.
2. Combine Ingredients in Blender:
   - In a blender, add the measured cooked and cooled carrots, 1/2 cup of low-fat plain yogurt, and 1 cup of almond milk.

3. Blend to Cake-Like Consistency:
 - Secure the blender lid and blend the ingredients on high until the mixture achieves a cake-like and smooth consistency. This typically takes about 1-2 minutes.

4. Check and Adjust Creaminess:
 - Pause and check the creaminess of the smoothie. If a silkier texture is desired, consider adding more almond milk gradually and blending again.

5. Serve with Delight:
 - Pour the Carrot Cake Concoction into a glass and savor its delightful flavors. Consider a sprinkle of cinnamon or a carrot slice as a garnish for an extra touch of indulgence.

Health Benefits for Diverticulitis:

- **Carrots' Dietary Fiber:** Cooked carrots provide dietary fiber, aiding in digestion and promoting regular bowel movements, which is beneficial for diverticulitis management.

- **Probiotic-Rich Plain Yogurt:** Low-fat plain yogurt introduces probiotics, supporting a healthy balance of gut flora and potentially alleviating digestive discomfort.

- **Nutty Almond Milk:** Almond milk provides a nutty essence to the mix, offering essential nutrients and dietary fiber that are gentle on the digestive system.

The Carrot Cake Concoction is more than a treat for your taste buds; it's a carefully blended creation designed to bring joy and support to individuals managing diverticulitis. Enjoy the delightful fusion of cooked carrots, plain yogurt, and almond milk with each sip, knowing you're nurturing your digestive health in a cake-like way.

Recipe 16: Gingered Pear Purity

Introduction:
The Gingered Pear Purity – a refreshing smoothie crafted to bring joy and digestive support to those managing diverticulitis. This unique blend combines the warming essence of fresh peeled ginger, the natural sweetness of ripe peeled pear, and the comforting embrace of low-fat vanilla yogurt. Beyond its invigorating taste, this smoothie is a thoughtful creation aimed at nurturing your digestive well-being.

Ingredients:
1. 1-inch Fresh Ginger (peeled)
2. 1 Ripe Pear (peeled)
3. 1/2 cup Low-fat Vanilla Yogurt

Instructions:

1. Prepare the Ingredients:
   - Peel and slice 1 inch of fresh ginger. Peel and dice a ripe pear, ensuring it's ready for blending.

2. Combine Ingredients in Blender:
   - In a blender, add the peeled and sliced fresh ginger, diced ripe pear, and 1/2 cup of low-fat vanilla yogurt.

3. Blend to Pure Perfection:
   - Secure the blender lid and blend the ingredients on high until the mixture achieves a pure and smooth consistency. This typically takes about 1-2 minutes.

4. Check and Adjust Freshness:
 - Pause and check the freshness of the smoothie. If a stronger ginger flavor is desired, consider adding more ginger and blending again.

5. Serve with Purity:
 - Pour the Gingered Pear Purity into a glass and savor its pure and invigorating flavors. Consider garnishing with a pear slice for an extra touch of elegance.

Health Benefits for Diverticulitis:

- **Ginger's Anti-Inflammatory Properties:** Fresh ginger is known for its anti-inflammatory properties, potentially easing digestive discomfort associated with diverticulitis.

- **Pear's Soluble Fiber:** Pears are rich in soluble fiber, aiding in softening stools and promoting regular bowel movements, which is beneficial for diverticulitis management.

- **Vanilla Yogurt's Digestive Comfort:** Low-fat vanilla yogurt offers a soothing quality, potentially easing digestive discomfort and introducing probiotics for gut health.

The Gingered Pear Purity is more than a refreshing beverage; it's a carefully blended creation designed to bring purity and support to individuals managing diverticulitis. Enjoy the invigorating fusion of fresh ginger, ripe pear, and vanilla yogurt with each sip, knowing you're nurturing your digestive health in a pure and delightful way.

Recipe 17: Cocoa Banana Bliss

Introduction:
Indulge in the blissful symphony of flavors with the Cocoa Banana Bliss – a rich and velvety smoothie created to bring delight and digestive support to those managing diverticulitis. This luscious blend features the natural sweetness of banana, the decadence of cocoa powder, the protein-rich allure of low-fat Greek yogurt, and the lightness of skim milk. Beyond its decadent taste, this smoothie is a thoughtfully crafted creation aimed at nurturing your digestive well-being.

Ingredients:
1. 1 Banana
2. 1 tablespoon Cocoa Powder
3. 1/2 cup Low-fat Greek Yogurt
4. 1 cup Skim Milk

Instructions:
1. Prepare the Banana:
   - Peel and slice the banana, ensuring it's ready for blending.
2. Add Cocoa Powder:
   - In a blender, add the sliced banana and 1 tablespoon of cocoa powder.

3. Include Greek Yogurt:
 - Add 1/2 cup of low-fat Greek yogurt to the blender for a creamy and protein-rich texture.

4. Pour in Skim Milk:
 - Measure 1 cup of skim milk and add it to the blender for a light and smooth consistency.

5. Blend to Blissful Consistency:
 - Secure the blender lid and blend the ingredients on high until the mixture achieves a blissful and smooth consistency. This typically takes about 1-2 minutes.

6. Check and Adjust Sweetness:
 - Pause and check the sweetness of the smoothie. If a sweeter taste is desired, consider adding a touch of honey or maple syrup and blending again.

7. Serve with Chocolatey Joy:
 - Pour the Cocoa Banana Bliss into a glass and savor its chocolatey joy. Consider a sprinkle of cocoa powder on top or a banana slice as a garnish for an extra touch of decadence.

Health Benefits for Diverticulitis:
- **Banana's Dietary Fiber:** Bananas provide dietary fiber, aiding in digestion and promoting regular bowel movements, which is beneficial for diverticulitis management.

- **Cocoa's Antioxidant Properties:** Cocoa powder contains antioxidants, potentially offering anti-inflammatory benefits that can support digestive health.

- **Protein-Packed Greek Yogurt:** Low-fat Greek yogurt adds a protein boost, supporting muscle health and providing a nutrient-dense element to the smoothie.

- **Light Skim Milk:** Skim milk provides a light and smooth texture without the excess fat, offering essential nutrients that are gentle on the digestive system.

The Cocoa Banana Bliss is not just a treat for your taste buds; it's a carefully crafted blend designed to bring joy and support to individuals managing diverticulitis. Enjoy the decadent fusion of banana, cocoa, Greek yogurt, and skim milk with each sip, knowing you're nurturing your digestive health in a blissful way.

Recipe 18: Plum Perfect Symphony

Introduction:
Embark on a symphony of perfection with the Plum Perfect Symphony – a smoothie created to bring both delight and digestive support to those managing diverticulitis. This harmonious blend features the natural sweetness of pitted plums, the protein-rich embrace of low-fat ricotta cheese, and the nutty richness of soy milk. Beyond its delightful taste, this smoothie is thoughtfully crafted to nurture your digestive well-being.

Ingredients:
1. 1 cup Pitted Plums
2. 1/2 cup Low-fat Ricotta Cheese
3. 1 cup Soy Milk

Instructions:

1. Prepare the Plums:
   - Pit and slice plums, ensuring they are ready for blending. Measure 1 cup of these pitted plums.

2. Combine Ingredients in Blender:
   - In a blender, add the measured pitted plums, 1/2 cup of low-fat ricotta cheese, and 1 cup of soy milk.

3. Blend to Perfect Symphony:
  - Secure the blender lid and blend the ingredients on high until the mixture achieves a perfect and smooth consistency. This typically takes about 1-2 minutes.

4. Check and Adjust Creaminess:
  - Pause and check the creaminess of the smoothie. If a silkier texture is desired, consider adding more soy milk gradually and blending again.

5. Serve with Plum Perfection:
  - Pour the Plum Perfect Symphony into a glass and savor its perfect blend of flavors. Consider garnishing with a plum slice for an extra touch of elegance.

Health Benefits for Diverticulitis:
- **Plums' Dietary Fiber:** Pitted plums are rich in dietary fiber, aiding in digestion and promoting regular bowel movements, which is beneficial for diverticulitis management.

- **Protein-Rich Ricotta Cheese:** Low-fat ricotta cheese adds a protein boost, supporting muscle health and providing a nutrient-dense element to the smoothie.

- **Nutty Soy Milk:** Soy milk provides a nutty richness to the mix, offering essential nutrients and dietary fiber that are gentle on the digestive system.

The Plum Perfect Symphony is more than a melody of flavors; it's a carefully orchestrated blend designed to bring joy and support to individuals managing diverticulitis. Enjoy the harmonious fusion of pitted plums, ricotta cheese, and soy milk with each sip, knowing you're nurturing your digestive health in a perfect way.

Recipe 19: Turmeric Ginger Tranquility

Introduction:
The Turmeric Ginger Tranquility – a soothing smoothie meticulously crafted to bring calm and digestive support to those managing diverticulitis. This serene blend features the anti-inflammatory warmth of fresh peeled and grated turmeric, the soothing essence of fresh peeled ginger, the protein-rich allure of low-fat Greek yogurt, and the hydrating touch of coconut water. Beyond its calming taste, this smoothie is thoughtfully designed to nurture your digestive well-being.

Ingredients:
1. 1-inch Fresh Turmeric (peeled and grated)
2. 1-inch Fresh Ginger (peeled)
3. 1/2 cup Low-fat Greek Yogurt
4. 1 cup Coconut Water

Instructions:
1. Prepare Turmeric and Ginger:
   - Peel and grate 1 inch of fresh turmeric. Peel 1 inch of fresh ginger. Both should be ready for blending.

2. Combine Ingredients in Blender:
   - In a blender, add the grated fresh turmeric, peeled fresh ginger, 1/2 cup of low-fat Greek yogurt, and 1 cup of coconut water.

3. Blend to Tranquil Consistency:
   - Secure the blender lid and blend the ingredients on high until the mixture achieves a tranquil and smooth consistency. This typically takes about 1-2 minutes.

4. Check and Adjust Freshness:
   - Pause and check the freshness of the smoothie. If a stronger ginger or turmeric flavor is desired, consider adding more ginger or turmeric gradually and blending again.

5. Serve with Tranquil Bliss:
   - Pour the Turmeric Ginger Tranquility into a glass and savor its serene flavors. Consider a sprinkle of ground turmeric or a ginger slice as a garnish for an extra touch of tranquility.

Health Benefits for Diverticulitis:
- **Turmeric's Anti-Inflammatory Properties:** Fresh turmeric contains curcumin, known for its anti-inflammatory properties that may help alleviate digestive discomfort associated with diverticulitis.

- **Ginger's Soothing Essence:** Ginger offers a soothing quality, potentially easing digestive discomfort and providing a calming effect on the digestive system.

- **Protein-Packed Greek Yogurt:** Low-fat Greek yogurt introduces probiotics, supporting gut health and potentially alleviating digestive discomfort.

- **Hydrating Coconut Water:** Coconut water provides hydration, ensuring a gentle and refreshing base for the smoothie.

The Turmeric Ginger Tranquility is more than a sip; it's a carefully blended creation designed to bring calm and support to individuals managing diverticulitis. Enjoy the soothing fusion of fresh turmeric, ginger, Greek yogurt, and coconut water with each sip, knowing you're nurturing your digestive health in a tranquil way.

Recipe 20: Cinnamon Apple Delight

Introduction:

Savor the warmth of a delightful experience with the Cinnamon Apple Delight – a comforting smoothie crafted to bring joy and digestive support to those managing diverticulitis. This delightful blend combines the sweetness of peeled apple slices, the cozy aroma of ground cinnamon, the probiotic richness of low-fat vanilla yogurt, and the creamy allure of oat milk. Beyond its comforting taste, this smoothie is thoughtfully designed to nurture your digestive well-being.

Ingredients:

1. 1 Apple (peeled and sliced)
2. 1/2 teaspoon Ground Cinnamon
3. 1/2 cup Low-fat Vanilla Yogurt
4. 1 cup Oat Milk

Instructions:

1. Prepare the Apple:
   - Peel and slice one apple, ensuring it's ready for blending.

2. Add Ground Cinnamon:
  - In a blender, add the peeled and sliced apple, 1/2 teaspoon of ground cinnamon, 1/2 cup of low-fat vanilla yogurt, and 1 cup of oat milk.

3. Blend to Applelicious Consistency:
  - Secure the blender lid and blend the ingredients on high until the mixture achieves an applelicious and smooth consistency. This typically takes about 1-2 minutes.

4. Check and Adjust Sweetness:
  - Pause and check the sweetness of the smoothie. If a sweeter taste is desired, consider adding a touch of honey or maple syrup and blending again.

5. Serve with Apple Delight:
  - Pour the Cinnamon Apple Delight into a glass and savor its delightful flavors. Consider a sprinkle of additional ground cinnamon or an apple slice as a garnish for an extra touch of coziness.

Health Benefits for Diverticulitis:
- **Apple's Dietary Fiber:** Apples are rich in soluble fiber, aiding in digestion and promoting regular bowel movements, which is beneficial for diverticulitis management.

- **Cinnamon's Anti-Inflammatory Properties:** Ground cinnamon contains antioxidants and anti-inflammatory properties, potentially offering digestive comfort and supporting overall well-being.

- **Probiotic-Rich Vanilla Yogurt:** Low-fat vanilla yogurt introduces probiotics, supporting gut health and potentially alleviating digestive discomfort.

- **Creamy Oat Milk:** Oat milk provides a creamy texture without the lactose, offering essential nutrients and dietary fiber that are gentle on the digestive system.

The Cinnamon Apple Delight is not just a sip; it's a carefully crafted blend designed to bring joy and support to individuals managing diverticulitis. Enjoy the comforting fusion of apple slices, ground cinnamon, vanilla yogurt, and oat milk with each sip, knowing you're nurturing your digestive health in a delightful way.

CONCLUSION

As we wrap up our journey through *"Smoothies for Diverticulitis,"* I want to extend my heartfelt gratitude for taking this adventure with me. Navigating the challenges of diverticulitis isn't easy, but I hope these smoothie recipes have brought a touch of joy and nourishment to your daily routine.

Remember, each sip was crafted with care, understanding the delicate balance our digestive systems crave. I've been in your shoes, felt the uncertainty around meal choices, and wanted to create something special – a collection of smoothies that not only ease the struggles but also celebrate the flavors life has to offer.

Whether it was the tropical delight or the cinnamon apple warmth, my goal was to make your culinary journey both health-conscious and enjoyable. Your well-being is at the heart of every recipe, and I hope these blends have become more than just beverages – they're your partners in digestive support.

But our journey doesn't end here. Keep experimenting, blending, and discovering what works best for you. Listen to your body, relish the flavors, and let each smoothie be a reminder that you're taking steps towards a healthier, happier you.

Thank you for letting me be a part of your kitchen, your routine, and your wellness journey. Here's to good health, delightful sips, and the empowering feeling of taking charge of your digestive well-being. Until we blend again, cheers to you!

THANK YOU FOR READING!

Thank you for your support on this culinary journey! If you enjoyed this book, please consider creating a video review or, if that's not feasible, leaving a written review. You can include a picture of the book or a page that caught your interest.

To leave a review, please scan the QR code below to access my author page, find the book, and share your thoughts. Your effort is greatly appreciated in spreading the joy of vibrant health and delicious living.

OTHER BOOKS BY THE SAME AUTHOR

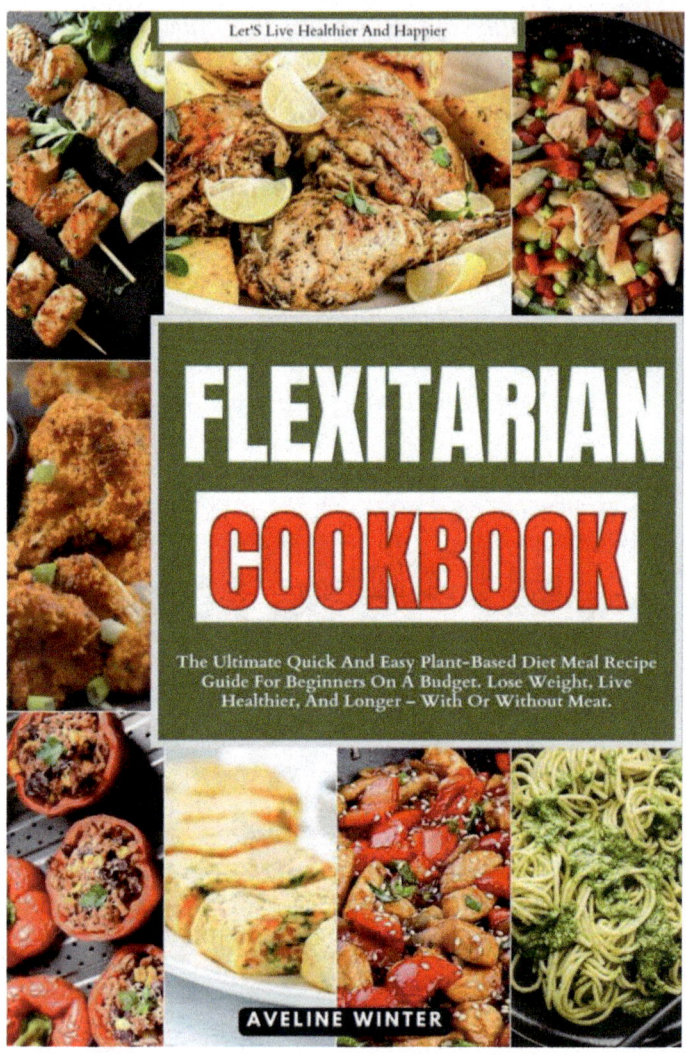

AVELINE WINTER

GASTRIC BYPASS
MEAL PLAN

The Complete 30-Day Bariatric Diet Designed to Help You Lose Weight and Live Healthier After Surgery.

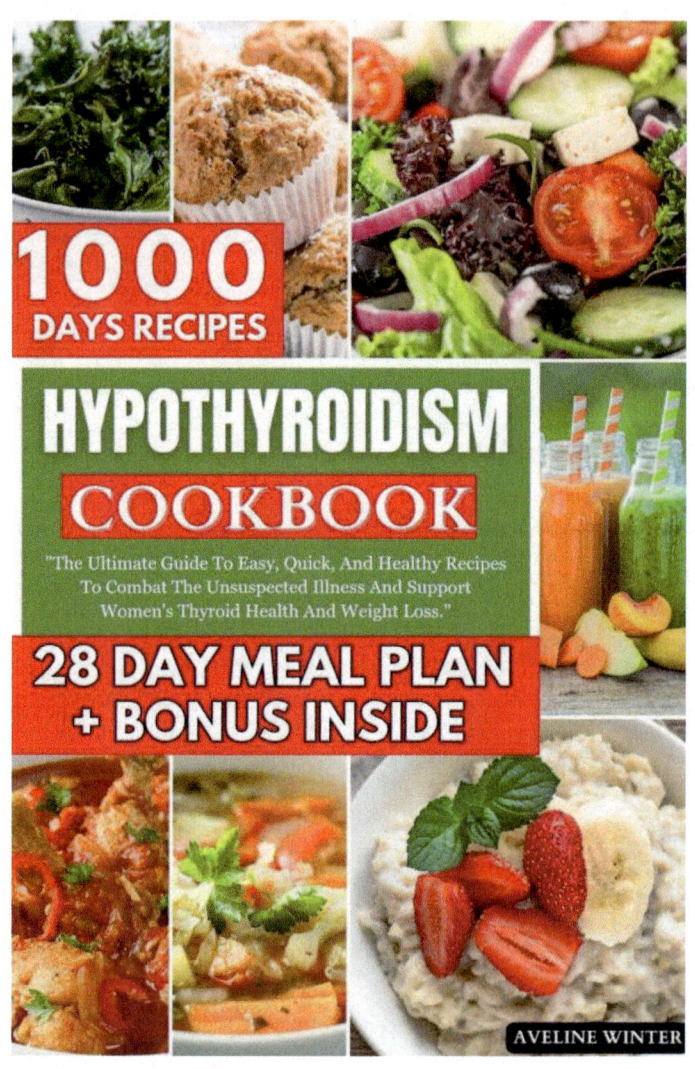

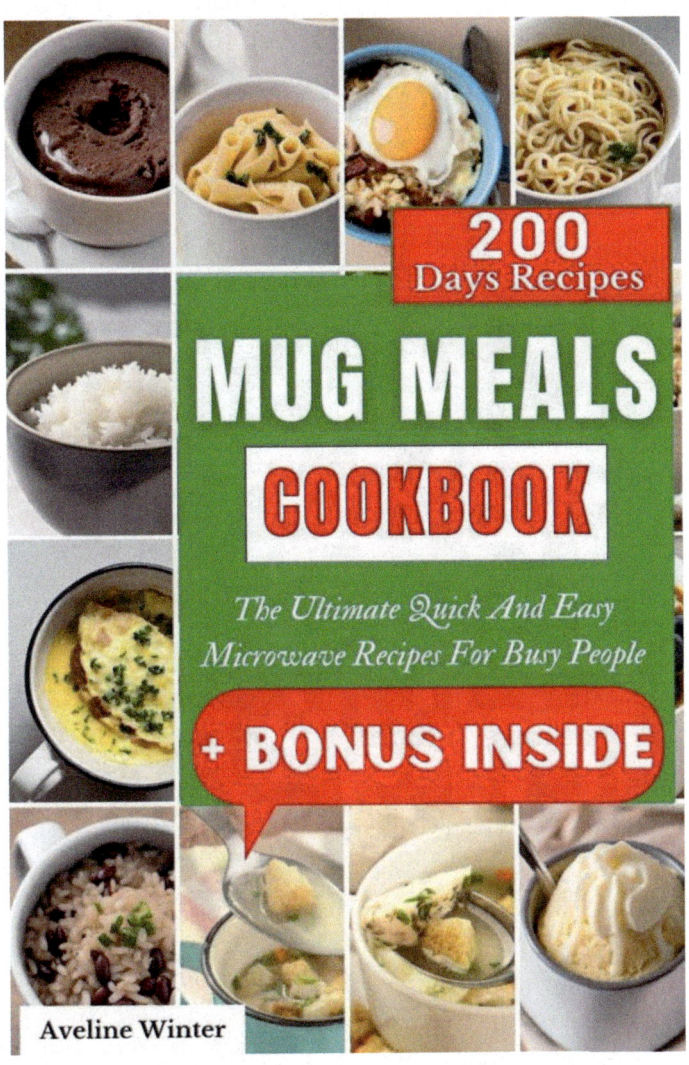

These books collectively offer over 1000 days worth of diverse and nourishing recipes tailored to specific dietary needs. Scan the QR code below to explore more amazing books created by Aveline Winter.

Please leave us a review to help others in need of this book locate it, we really appreciate your effort in spreading the word. Thank you once again!

Printed in Dunstable, United Kingdom

68533435R00047